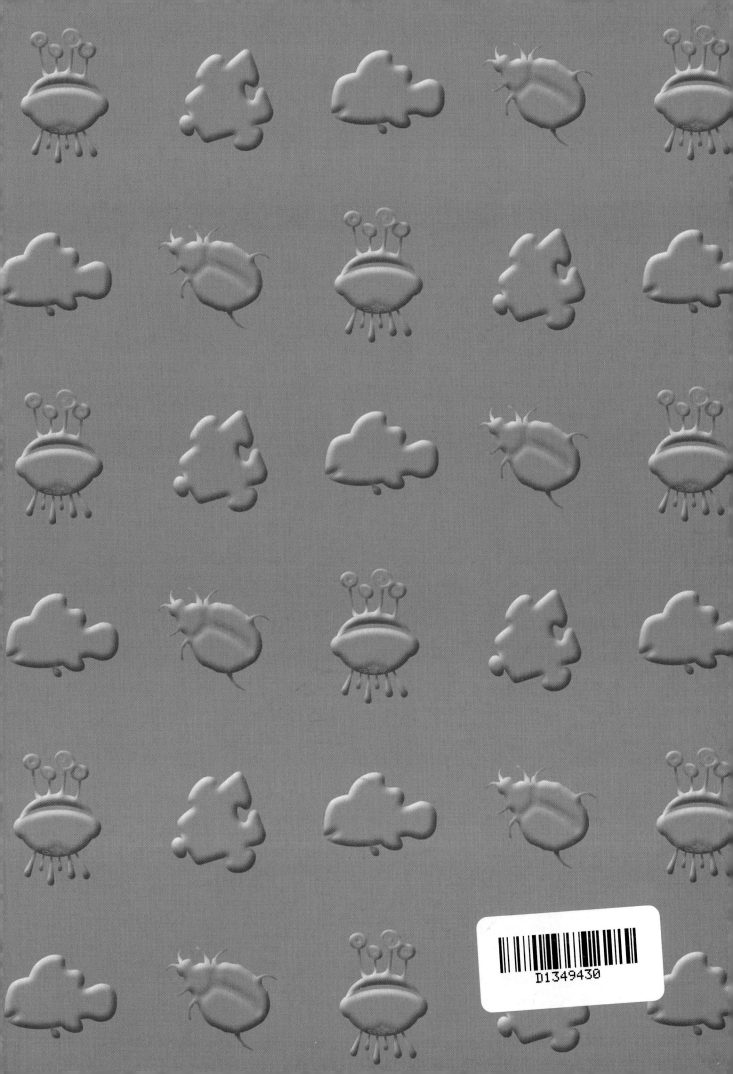

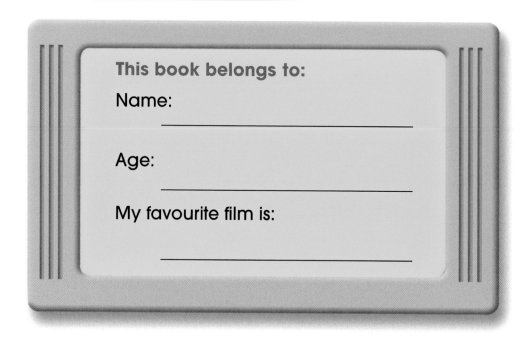

This book belongs to:

Name:

_____

Age:

_____

My favourite film is:

_____

Editor: Anne Ewart   Designer: Phil Williams

Published in Great Britain in 2004 by Egmont Books Limited,
239 Kensington High Street, London W8 6SA. Printed in Italy. ISBN 1-4052-1388-4
3 5 7 9 10 8 6 4 2

Note to parents: adult supervision is recommended when sharp-pointed items such as scissors are in use.

DISNEP·PIXAR

ANNUAL 2005

FROM TOY STORY TO FINDING NEMO

DISNEP·PIXAR
TOY STORY AND BEYOND!

DISNEP·PIXAR
FINDING NEMO

DISNEP·PIXAR
MONSTERS, INC.

DISNEP·PIXAR
a bug's life

DISNEY·PIXAR
ANNUAL 2005

CONTENTS

Disney·PIXAR MONSTERS, INC.

Disney·PIXAR FINDING NEMO

a bug's life

Disney·PIXAR TOY STORY AND BEYOND!

Celebrity Mike

One evening, Mike was waiting to see the Monsters, Inc. advert on TV. "Here it comes!" shouted Mike. But when the advert appeared, Mike's face was completely covered by the Monsters, Inc. logo. Sulley thought Mike would be upset but a big grin spread across Mike's green face. "Hurray! I've been on TV! I'm a real celebrity," he cheered.

Sulley wondered if Mike was just pretending to be happy in front of his friends. "Mike really wants to be famous, but things always seem to go wrong," thought Sulley.

The next day, Mr Waternoose announced that there was to be a huge advertisement campaign. "As my top scare team, you two will be the stars!" he told Mike and Sulley.

"I'm going to be a star!" screamed Mike. "The first phase is a giant poster on the side of the Monsters, Inc. building," said Mr Waternoose. Mike rushed outside to see it. Sulley groaned when he saw a big tree covering Mike's face on the poster. Mike didn't seem to notice. "I won't let fame go to my head," Mike told the other monsters.

"That's not all!" said Mr Waternoose, leading Sulley and Mike to the parking lot. "This gigantic hot air balloon will soon be floating over Monstropolis," he explained.

"Everyone in the city will see me. I'm going to make some calls and tell people to look up!" chuckled Mike. "At least this can't go wrong," thought Sulley, happily.

When the balloon went up, a little cloud hung right in front of Mike's face. Sulley sighed but Mike didn't even notice. "I might start charging for autographs," joked Mike. Sulley realised that everyone already knew Mike. "He's such a great guy, he doesn't need an advert to be a celebrity," thought Sulley, as he joined Mike's crowd of admirers.

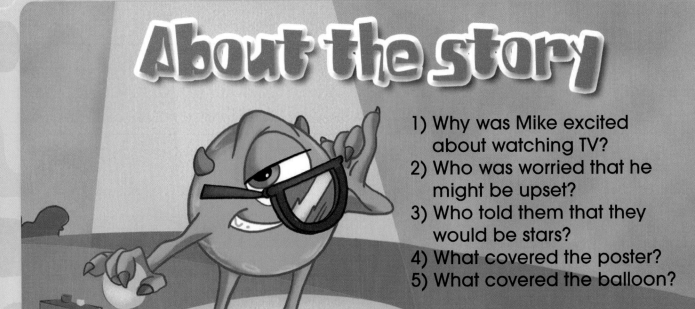

About the story

1) Why was Mike excited about watching TV?
2) Who was worried that he might be upset?
3) Who told them that they would be stars?
4) What covered the poster?
5) What covered the balloon?

Answers:
1) Because he was going to appear in an advert.
2) Sulley. 3) Mr Waternoose. 4) A tree. 5) A cloud.

Roar Score

Sulley has perfected his roaring technique! Use the code below to work out how many screams Sulley collected behind each door.

Behind which door did Sulley collect the most screams?

11

Make a monster

Monsters come in all shapes and sizes! Here's how you can make a short, scaly monster with one eye and horns!

You will need: a short bottle, netting, coloured card, modelling clay, scissors, sticky tape and glue.

1 Stick the netting onto the bottle with sticky tape.

2 Cut out an eye and two arms from the coloured card.

3 Glue them onto your monster.

12

4 Cut out some feet and a mouth from card and make some horns out of modelling clay.

5 Glue them onto your monster.

WHAT WILL YOUR NEXT MONSTER LOOK LIKE?

Spot the difference

These two pictures may look the same but there are ten differences in the bottom picture. Can you spot them all?

TO SCAREFLOORS

Answers: 1) Sulley's tail is missing. 2) Boo's costume's eye pupil is missing. 3) Mike's shadow has disappeared. 4) A CDA agent's air tube is missing. 5) A CDA agent's numbers are missing. 6) Mr Waternoose's bow tie is missing. 7) Mr Waternoose's waistcoat has changed colour. 8) The writing on the wall is missing. 9) A pair of clock hands are missing. 10) A CDA agent's eye holes are missing.

Colouring time

Mike and Sulley are best friends. Can you add some colour to this picture?

15

Personal taste

Sulley and Mike discover that being best friends does not necessarily mean that you like the same things!

One bright, chilly morning, Sulley and Mike were walking to work. Sulley felt very tired and he noticed that Mike kept yawning, too. "Did you have a bad night's sleep?" asked Sulley.

"The cold kept me awake. The blanket on my bed isn't very thick," replied Mike.

Suddenly, Mike noticed that Sulley was wearing a pair of dark glasses. "What's with the shades, Sulley?" asked Mike.

"Oh, I'm resting my eyes. The curtains in my room are too thin. They let in the light as soon as the sun comes up," explained Sulley.

That lunch-time, Sulley crept out of Monsters, Inc. and went to a department store on Monstropolis's high street. "I'll buy Mike a warm blanket, so he can get some sleep tonight," chuckled Sulley.

He couldn't decide what colour or pattern Mike would like, until he saw a big, blue blanket with bright, purple spots. "Hey, what a great-looking blanket. It's just like my fur," said Sulley.

Meanwhile, Mike had crept out to another store. "I'll buy my buddy Sulley some thick curtains to keep the sun out of his room," chuckled Mike.

He knew exactly which ones he wanted to buy for Sulley. "Green is my favourite colour. These will look great in Sulley's room," decided Mike.

When Sulley and Mike met again at work, they produced their gifts. "Surprise!" they announced, at exactly the same time.

Mike gulped when he saw the blanket Sulley had bought him. He didn't like the colour, or the pattern, but he didn't want to seem ungrateful, so he pretended that he really liked it. "Wow, blue with purple spots! I can't wait to get it home," fibbed Mike.

Sulley liked the green curtains even less. But Mike seemed so happy with the blanket, that Sulley pretended he was happy with the curtains. "They'll look really great hanging in my room," lied Sulley.

That night, the spotty blanket made Mike feel dizzy, while the green curtains gave Sulley a headache.

The next morning, they both looked even more tired.

"How was the new blanket?" asked Sulley.

"Erm ... it was really ... interesting. How were the curtains?" replied Mike.

"They certainly made me forget about the sunshine," said Sulley.

But Sulley didn't want to keep pretending, so he decided to tell Mike the truth. "Mike, it's about the curtains ..." started Sulley.

Mike broke down and covered his eye with his hands. "Please don't thank me again. I can't stand the blanket you gave me!" he cried.

"Phew! Thank goodness for that. I think the curtains you chose look terrible," giggled Sulley.

They both laughed when they realised that they had each picked colours that they would like for themselves.

Just then, Sulley had a thought. "Those green curtains would make two very warm blankets!" he said.

"And that big, thick blanket you gave me would make a fantastic curtain," replied Mike.

So the two friends exchanged their gifts and that night they both had the best night's sleep, ever!

Top Scarer

Play this game with a friend to find out who can join Sulley and Mike at Monsters, Inc. as part of their Top Scarer team!

You will need: a pen and 16 small pieces of paper.

Player 1

Player 2

Player 1	Player 2
10	10
9	9
8	8
7	7
6	6
5	5
4	4
3	3
2	2
1	1

How to play

Decide who will be Player 1 and who will be Player 2. Cover each of the numbers in the circles below with a piece of paper. Take it in turns to pick up two pieces of paper. If the numbers match, keep the pieces of paper and colour in this number of sections on your scream-o-meter. If the numbers don't match, put the pieces of paper back again. The first person to colour in all 10 sections of their scream-o-meter can join the Top Scarer team!

3 1 2 3

3 2 3 1

2 1 3 1

1 2 1 3

19

Sock alert!

Which path do the CDA agents need to take to reach the sock on George's back?

CAUTION! SOCK ALERT!
Monsters, Inc.

Answer: b

Hiding Randall

Randall can blend into any background. How many times can you find Randall on this page?

Answer: Nine.

21

JESSIE'S JOKES!

Why don't aliens starve in space?
They can find a mars and a milky way!

What fish swims only at night?
A starfish!

What do insects learn at school?
Mothmatics!

What is the best way to communicate with a fish?
Drop it a line!

How do you know if Sulley is under your bed?
You bump your nose on the ceiling!

Which part of a fish weighs the most?
The scales!

Why was the big, hairy, two-headed monster top of the class at school?
Because two heads are better than one!

Which fish go to heaven when they die?
Angelfish!

What do you get if you cross some ants with some tics?
All sorts of antics!

Why are horses bad dancers?
They have two left feet!

How does a robot shave?
With a laser blade!

What holds up the moon?
Moonbeams!

Why are spiders like tops?
They are always spinning!

Back to Front

One morning, Mr Ray glided into school and announced that the whole class would be going on a field trip. "OK, everyone, climb on board," said Mr Ray. "Let's sit at the back," said Sheldon. "Why?" asked Nemo. "Mr Ray won't be able to see us and we can have some fun," said Sheldon. "Only the teacher's pet sits at the front of the class."

They took off and Mr Ray skimmed over the top of some glittering coral. He began to tell the class facts about all the interesting plants and wonderful creatures that lived there.

Nemo and his friends at the back weren't listening though; they were too busy chatting. As they passed an old crab, Sheldon poked out his tongue and made his friends laugh.

Then the gang started playing a game where they took turns tugging the tail of a fish in front of them. Every time the angry fish turned around, they said it wasn't them.

They were giggling so much that some of their classmates asked them to be quiet. "We can't hear Mr Ray," they complained, but that just made the gang laugh even more.

When the field trip was over, Mr Ray made an announcement. "Now, I want each of you to tell the rest of the class what you learned today," he told them.

One by one, the little fish talked about the interesting seaweed and shells they had seen that day. When it was Nemo and his friends' turn, they had nothing to say.

"That's because you were all too busy playing at the back of the class," frowned Mr Ray. Nemo felt sad because they had missed out on seeing all the interesting things.

"Don't worry, kids, we're going on another field trip tomorrow," smiled Mr Ray. The next day, Nemo and his friends sat right at the front and they had even more fun than before.

About the story

1) Who was taking the class on the field trip?
2) Where did Sheldon suggest they sit?
3) What did Sheldon do to the old crab?
4) Why was the fish in front of them angry?
5) Where did Nemo sit on the next field trip?

26

Puzzle time

Join in with Nemo and Squirt's fun by finding the answers to these three teasers.

1

How many times can you find Nemo's name in the jumble below?

Nemo Nemo Nemo Nemo Nemo Nemo Nemo

2

Can you join the dots to find a type of fish?

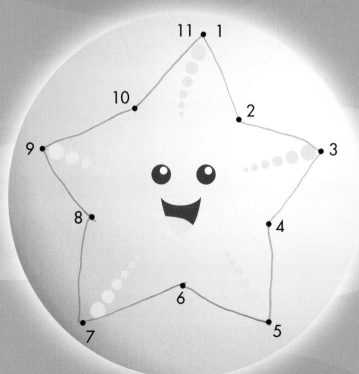

3

Can you put these lengths of seaweed in order, longest first?

a b c d e

27

Dory's whale friend

Dory has great fun speaking 'whale' to her whale friends. Here's how you can make your own whale to talk to!

You will need: a square of blue paper, scissors, white paper, black pen and glue.

1 Fold a square of blue paper in half, diagonally. Unfold, then fold the two opposite sides over so that they meet at the fold.

2 Fold the tip over to meet the centre fold.

3 Fold the shape in half, then fold the tail up.

4 Make a short cut through the end of the fold in the tail. Fold the edges of the tail outwards.

5 Cut an eye from white paper and draw on an eyeball. Stick it onto your whale.

WHAT WILL YOU SAY TO YOUR WHALE?

Eye-Spy!

Can you draw a wiggly line to match each sea creature on this page to its close-up? To whom does the extra close-up belong?

30

Bruce's bite

Can you discover what Bruce is searching for? Colour in the squares whose co-ordinates appear in the list below to find out.

1b, 1c, 1d, 1e, 1f, 2d, 2f, 4b, 4c, 4d, 4e, 4f, 6b, 6d, 6e, 6f, 7b, 7c, 7d, 7f, 9b, 9c, 9d, 9e, 9f, 10d, 11b, 11c, 11d, 11e, 11f

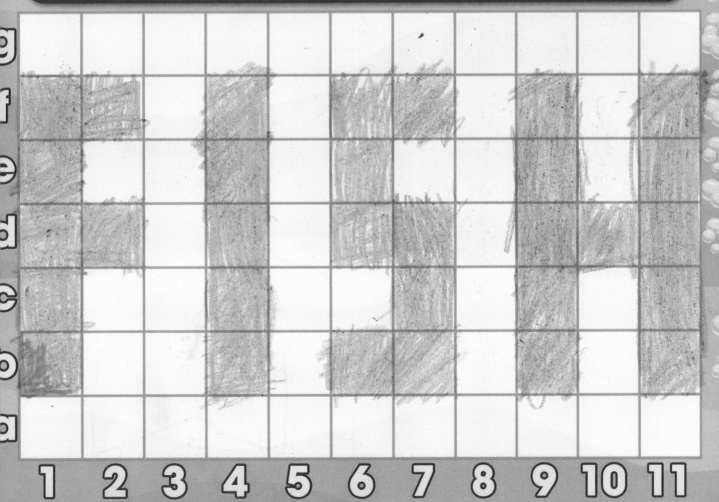

ANSWER: FISH.

The new teacher

Dory reminds Marlin that he knows much more than he could ever have imagined!

It was very unusual for Marlin to oversleep but this morning Marlin had overslept by thirty minutes!

"Wake up, Nemo! Wake up!" he shouted as he jumped into action.

"Just five more minutes' sleep, Dad! Please," sighed Nemo as he rolled over.

"No, Nemo," said Marlin. "You must get up now! You're late for school!"

Nemo gasped and his eyelids sprang open. "I can't be late for school today!" he cried. "Mr Ray is taking us on a trip and he'll be teaching us lots of cool, new things!"

Nemo rushed to school as quickly as he could. But it was too late. Mr Ray had already left, with Nemo's class swimming along on his back.

"No! Come back!" shouted Nemo after them. But no one heard him. Mr Ray and the class were gone for the day and there was nothing Nemo could do about it.

"I'm sorry, Nemo!" said Marlin. "I shouldn't have let you oversleep. How can I make it up to you?"

Nemo just shrugged, disappointed. He was so upset to be missing out on all the new things.

"I know," said Marlin, excitedly. "I can be your teacher for the day!" He was rather pleased that he'd come up with a plan.

"But Mr Ray makes everything so much fun, Dad," replied Nemo.

"Fun? I bet I can make teaching more fun than Mr Ray," said Marlin.

Nemo wasn't convinced, but he swam off with his father to see what he could learn.

Marlin was having great fun playing the teacher.

Suddenly, a huge school of fish swam overhead. "Now, Nemo," said Marlin in his best teacher voice. "These wonderful creatures are called fish."

"Dad!" sighed Nemo. "I know what fish are. We're fish."

"Hmm," said Marlin. "This is going to be harder than I thought."

Everywhere they went, Marlin pointed out one creature after another – starfish, seahorses, dolphins. But Nemo knew about them all.

Just then, Dory arrived. "What are you two doing?" she asked.

"Dad's trying to be my teacher but he doesn't know **anything** new," said Nemo, sadly.

"Has he told you about starfish?" asked Dory, excitedly.

Nemo's heart sank.

Dory continued, "Oh, oh! And what about that ugly thing with a great big light hanging down in front of its face? Remember, Marlin?"

"Dory, fish don't need lights," huffed Nemo.

"They do when they live at the bottom of the deepest part of the ocean because it is so dark down there," said Marlin.

Nemo was entranced by what his father had to say. "Wow, Dad! You **are** a great teacher, after all!" cried Nemo. He couldn't wait to tell his class all about it the next day!

Colouring time

Nemo likes listening to Nigel's tales. Can you add some bright colours to the scene?

Deep-sea shadows

Can you match each shadow with its correct character name?

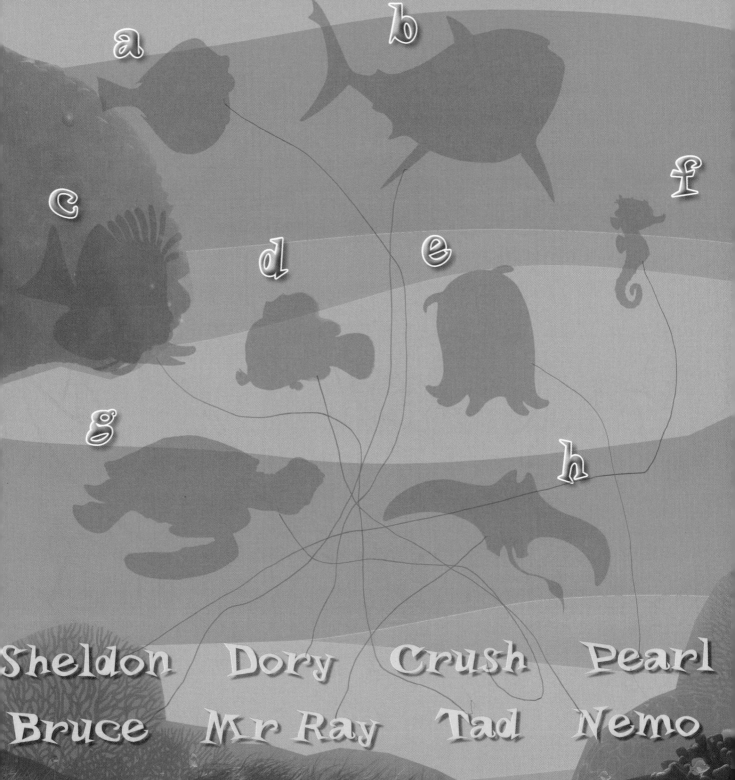

a   b

c

f

d   e

g

h

Sheldon   Dory   Crush   Pearl

Bruce   Mr Ray   Tad   Nemo

Answers: a - Dory, b - Bruce, c - Tad, d - Nemo, e - Pearl, f - Sheldon, g - Crush, h - Mr Ray

35

Colour Dory

Dory is very excited to find out that her pictures are going to be coloured in. Play this game with a friend to find out who will finish first!

You will need: a dice and coloured pencils.

Player 1

36

How to play

Take it in turns to roll the dice and colour in the part of Dory that matches the number on the dice. If there is nothing left to colour of that number, you must wait for your next turn. The first person to colour in all of Dory is the winner! Why not play again by tracing Dory's outline onto another piece of paper?

Player 2

Spot the difference

Answers: 1) Gill's eyes are different. 2) Letter 't' on sign is missing. 3) Nemo is missing. 4) Colour of rock has changed. 5) Bubbles the fish has moved. 6) Extra rock. 7) Colour of leaf. 8) Bars missing on helmet. 9) Gill's fin is in a different position. 10) One of Deb's white stripes is missing.

Grab shell, dude!

Dory and Marlin need to reach Crush quickly to travel along the East Australian Current. Can you help them?

Start

Finish

39

TRUE OR FALSE?

Can you work out which of these film facts are true and which are false?

1 Buzz originally thought that he worked for Star Fleet.

2 Woody was stolen by a man called Al.

3 Monsters, Inc. is in Scaretropolis.

4 Marlin and Dory were swallowed by a dolphin.

5 Sulley is Top Scarer at Monsters, Inc.

10 Hopper is afraid of beetles.

11 Bruce's shark buddies are called Chum and Anchor.

6 Flik and the ant colony live on Bug Island.

12 Sulley names the little girl he meets Goo.

7 The toys used traffic cones to help them cross the road.

8 Dot is leader of the Blueberry Troop.

9 Nemo was taken from the ocean and put into a teacher's fish tank.

Problem solved

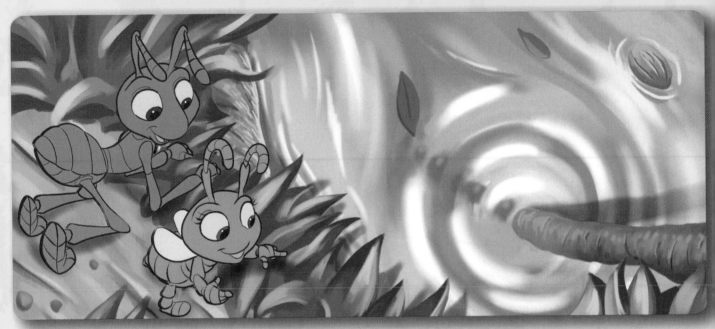

Flik and Dot were at the edge of Ant Island. Flik noticed that lots of grain had fallen into the river. "All that grain going to waste," said Flik. "But ants don't like water," said Dot.

"There's always a way to solve a problem," replied Flik. Dot spotted a twig at the water's edge. "We can climb down this twig and grab the grain as it floats past," said Dot.

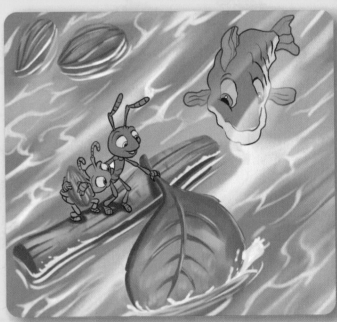

But when Dot climbed onto the twig and grabbed a grain, the twig slid into the water. "Oh no!" cried Dot, as the twig started to float away from Ant Island.

"Don't worry, Dot!" cried Flik, and he leaped onto the twig behind her. Quickly, Flik grabbed a leaf that was floating on the water and dragged it onto the twig.

Flik held the leaf up and used it as a sail. The wind started to blow them back towards Ant Island. "Problem solved," laughed Flik. "**And** we collected some grain," laughed Dot.

But before long, the wind changed direction and Flik and Dot were blown away from Ant Island. "We'll have to think of something else," said Flik, as he lowered the leaf.

Just then, a fish tried to snatch the grain from Dot's hand. "Careful!" cried Flik. Suddenly, he had an idea. "I think that fish will be able to give us a ride home," said Flik.

Carefully, Flik peeled a soft strand of bark from the twig and tied it to the grain. The fish grabbed hold of the grain and swam off. "Hold on tight!" chuckled Flik.

As the fish pulled them across the river, Dot held the leaf in the water and scooped up all the floating grain. When the fish passed close to Ant Island, Flik let go of the strand of bark and set the fish free. The twig, with Dot and Flik on it, sailed smoothly into shore. "Well done, Dot. We make a great team!" laughed Flik. "Problem solved!" giggled Dot.

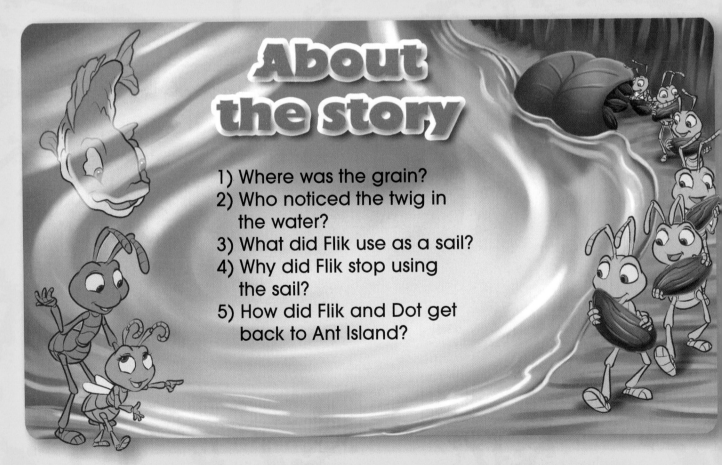

About the story

1) Where was the grain?
2) Who noticed the twig in the water?
3) What did Flik use as a sail?
4) Why did Flik stop using the sail?
5) How did Flik and Dot get back to Ant Island?

Answers:
1) In the river. 2) Dot. 3) A leaf. 4) Because the wind changed direction. 5) They were pulled back by a fish.

Bug talk

How well do you know Flik and his friends? Draw a line to match each character with its saying. Give yourself two points for each correct answer and see how well you score.

1

2

3

4

5

a I hate performing on an empty stomach!

b We could get bigger bugs to fight the grasshoppers! I'll go to the City to find them!

c Let's ride!

d The ants pick the food, the ants keep the food and the grasshoppers ... leave!

e Not until my wings grow in!

Score

4 or less - Watch the film again and have another go.
6 or 8 - Well done. You know Flik and his friends very well.
10 - Fantastic. You're a bug expert!

Answers: 1-b, 2-c, 3-e, 4-a, 5-d

Colouring time

Flik is teaching Hopper a lesson! Can you add some colour to the picture?

Heimlich's hunt

Heimlich is playing hide-and-seek with his friends but he's much too hungry to concentrate! Can you help him work out who is hiding behind each leaf?

Rosie

Slim

Francis

Dim

Answers: a – Francis, b – Rosie, c – Slim, d – Dim.

47

Food fight

Can Heimlich's hunger help him to save his friends from an even hungrier toad?

PT Flea and his circus troop were on their way to a new location. "I know where there's a rotten old tree stump. It's crawling with bugs just waiting to be entertained," chuckled PT Flea, as he steered the circus trailer through the long grass.

"I'm hungry. Can we stop and find something delicious to eat?" asked Heimlich.

"This could be our biggest gig ever, and all you can think of is food?" cried PT Flea.

"I perform better when I'm full," replied Heimlich.

"I'm not waiting. But you can grab a bite and catch us up if you like," grumbled PT Flea.

Heimlich climbed off the trailer and looked around. He gasped when he looked up and saw a huge apple hanging from a tree.

"Yum, yum," drooled Heimlich as he crawled up the tree to reach it.

Meanwhile, the circus troop had reached the tree stump. "We'll

set up here," said PT Flea.

But a hungry toad had heard them arrive and was hopping towards the trailer.

"My, my ... a meal on wheels," sniggered the toad.

"Quick! Everyone back inside the trailer," yelled PT Flea.

The circus troop only just managed to clamber back into the trailer in time.

"Leave us alone ... or ... or you'll be sorry," called out Francis.

"Food can't fight back," gurgled the toad.

But at that moment, Heimlich looked down from the tree. "Oh dear. My friends are in trouble!" he gasped when he saw the toad.

"Heimlich! Help us, or we'll become snacks!" yelled PT Flea.

The whole troop groaned when they saw Heimlich shuffle towards an apple. "Even at a time like this, he is still thinking about food!" said PT Flea.

But Heimlich had a plan. He began munching on an apple stalk.

The toad had just squeezed its big mouth through the door of the trailer, when an apple dropped down and thumped onto its back.

Before the toad had a chance to recover, a second apple landed on its head. The toad hopped away under a shower of falling apples.

"Well done, Heimlich! You proved that food **can** fight back," cheered Francis.

Suddenly the troop heard clapping. A huge audience had watched the whole thing.

"If you thought that was good, wait until you see the rest of our show!" declared PT Flea.

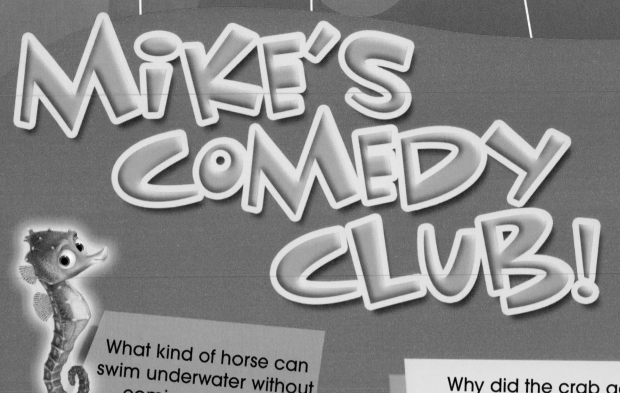

MIKE'S COMEDY CLUB!

What kind of horse can swim underwater without coming up for air?
A seahorse!

Why did the crab get arrested?
Because he was always pinching things!

What do whales eat?
Fish and ships!

How do you greet 3-headed monste
Hello, hello, hello

What is even bigge
that an eleph-ant?
A gi-ant!

50

Where do you weigh whales?
At a whale-weigh station!

What has four wheels and flies?
A rubbish bin!

What is an insect's favourite game?
Cricket!

Where do fish wash?
In a river basin!

What happens if a big, hairy monster sits in front of you at the cinema?
You miss most of the film!

What do you call a dinosaur that wears a cowboy hat and boots?
Tyrannosaurus tex!

What did the astronaut cook for lunch?
An unidentified frying object!

What do astronauts wear to keep warm?
Apollo-neck sweaters!

The silent search

Buzz and the toys were inside Al's Toy Barn, searching for Woody. "There might be a security guard in here, so it's important that we all keep very quiet," Buzz told the group.

But as soon as the toys started to walk along the aisle, Mr Potato Head's shoes began to squeak very loudly on the shiny floor. "Shhh," whispered Buzz.

Mr Potato Head tried walking on his tip-toes. But then Hamm's trotters began making a tapping sound on the floor. "Am I the only professional here?" sighed Buzz.

"I'll keep Hamm quiet," said Rex, and he gave Hamm a piggy-back. But just then, when the toys turned into the next aisle, Slinky's spring was yanked sideways!

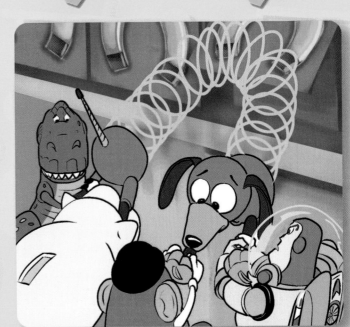

"Help! I'm stuck to a magnet," cried Slinky. "I don't believe this! We've only been here for five minutes and we're already one man down!" groaned Buzz.

Buzz tried to pull Slinky free, but the magnet was too strong. "Give me a hand, guys," puffed Buzz. The toys all pulled and Slinky flew off, landing on the floor with a clang!

"Shhhh!" cried everybody. Slinky and the toys carried on walking, but all the pulling had stretched Slinky's spring. It dragged along, jangling like a bell. "We'll never find Woody if we can't be quiet," said Buzz. "But we're only quiet when we're standing still," replied Hamm. Then Buzz spotted a skateboard hanging up in the aisle and had an idea.

"Everyone climb on and don't move," ordered Buzz. He grabbed a magnet and jumped on in front of them. Then Buzz pointed the magnet towards a metal bin and told everyone to hold on tight. The power of the magnet made the skateboard glide silently along the floor. "Now we can look for Woody without making any noise," grinned Buzz.

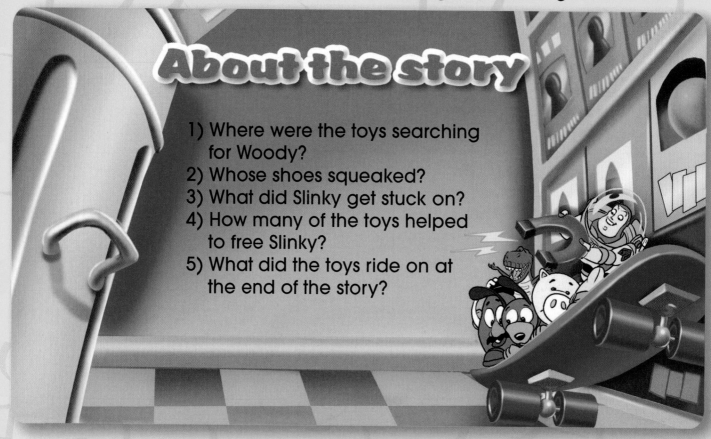

About the story

1) Where were the toys searching for Woody?
2) Whose shoes squeaked?
3) What did Slinky get stuck on?
4) How many of the toys helped to free Slinky?
5) What did the toys ride on at the end of the story?

Answers:
1) Al's Toy Barn. 2) Mr Potato Head's. 3) A magnet. 4) All of them (four). 5) A skateboard.

Best buddies

Buzz and Woody always know how to
have a good time when they're together!

1 Which of the words below
can't be made from the letters
in Buzz Lightyear's name?

trail   light   great
bright   learnt

2 How many cowboy hats
can you find in this mix-up?

3 Finish drawing the
under-side of the space-
ship, then colour it in.

55

Colouring time

Help the alien put Mr Potato Head back together by adding some colours.

56

Toy teasers

There's always something going on when the toys are in town. See if you can answer each of these teasers.

1 Can you match Bullseye to his correct shadow ?

a   b   c

d   e   f

2 How many coins has Hamm found?

3 Unscramble the letters below to find out what Rex likes playing.

idevo mesag

57

Ready, set, go!

Buzz and his friends are on an exciting adventure to rescue Woody. Play this game with your friends to see who will be the champion cone carrier.

How to play

You will need: a dice and a counter for each player.

Place all the counters at Start, next to Buzz. Take it in turns to roll the dice and move your counter along the path the number of spaces shown on the dice. If you land on a *drop* space, miss a turn. If you land on a *go* space, throw again. The first person to reach Woody is the winner! Watch out for the sticky, pink chewing gum!

29 | 30 | 31 | drop

sPlat!
Go back to Start

27

33

go

34

25

35

24

36

P 23

37

Finish

38 | drop | 40

Alien encounter

You have been chosen to join in with the aliens' fun. Look closely and count how many there are of each alien. Which alien appears the most number of times?

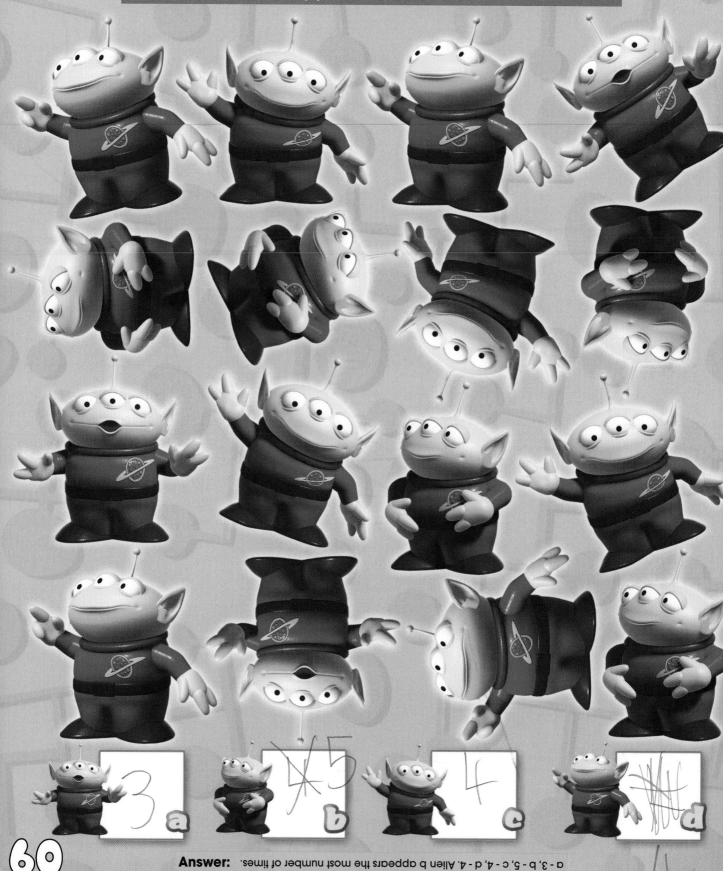

Answer: a - 3, b - 5, c - 4, d - 4. Alien b appears the most number of times.

Woody's roundup

Woody knows that it takes a lot of skill to be a true cowboy. Can you help him round up the answers to these puzzles?

1 Can you match each of these cowboy objects to their correct name?

a   b   c   d   e

badge   spur   hat   boot   saddle

2 Which of Woody's three friends is the tallest? Which is the shortest?

3 Cross off all the letters that appear twice. The remaining letters will spell the name of Woody's best friend.

61

Building team

Mr Potato Head learns that sometimes working as a team is the best way to get something done!

It was an exciting day for the toys. Andy had been given a new box of building bricks and the toys couldn't wait to play with them.

When Andy left the house, the toys tipped the box of bricks out onto the carpet. "Let's build a car!" said Mr Potato Head.

"I think we should build a dinosaur!" said Rex.

No one could agree what they should build, so everyone began building different things.

Before long, Mr Potato Head had nearly finished building his car but he needed just one more brick.

He looked around and saw that Rex had some bricks left so he crept onto the window ledge and stole one of them.

"Hey, I'm using that," cried Rex, as he grabbed the brick back.

Mr Potato Head and Rex began tugging at the brick. Neither would let the brick go.

Suddenly, Mr Potato Head's arm came off and he tumbled backwards out of the open window.

"Oh my goodness!" cried Rex. "Mr Potato Head's fallen into the garden!"

The toys rushed

onto the window ledge and looked down into the garden.

They were all very relieved to see that Mr Potato Head had managed to grab onto the washing line. "Help me, guys, or I'll end up as mashed potato!" he gulped.

"We've got to go down to the garden and rescue him," said Buzz.

"But the washing line is far too high for us to reach," said Jessie.

"I feel terrible. This is all because we were arguing over a building brick," groaned Rex.

"That's it! We can use the bricks," said Woody. "If we work as a team, we can save Mr Potato Head and all be back here before Andy gets home."

Leading the way, Buzz crept into the corridor to check that the coast was clear. Then the toys each took a brick and made their way down the stairs, and out into the garden.

They all looked up and saw Mr Potato Head, dangling high above them. "I don't know how much longer my arm will stay on," groaned Mr Potato Head.

"We've got to work quickly," said Buzz.

The toys began building a tower with the bricks. With everyone working together, it wasn't long before they reached Mr Potato Head and helped him down.

"Well done, team. We can do anything when we work together," said Buzz.

"Thanks, guys. I'm sorry I took your brick, Rex," apologised Mr Potato Head.

"No problem. Maybe we could build a dinosaur-car together?" giggled Rex.

The toys all laughed, as they took the tower down and carried the building bricks back up to Andy's room.

63

Space defender

Buzz is always ready to battle the evil Emperor Zurg. Here's how you can make your own spaceships to take into battle!

You will need: a square of brightly coloured paper, some white paper, scissors and glue.

1 Fold your square of coloured paper in half and open it again so you can see the crease. Fold one corner into the middle so the edge meets the crease. Do the same with the other corner.

2 Keeping the folds you have made in place, fold the same corners down into the middle again.

3 Fold the plane in half inwards, along the centre fold you first made. On each side, fold the top corner down to make a wing.

4 Draw a Buzz Lightyear flash on the white paper. Cut it out and glue it onto your spaceship.

5 Now make a spaceship for Zurg.

LET THE BATTLE BEGIN!

Zurg zone

The evil Emperor Zurg is an old meany but he can't stop you from having fun!

1 Following the sequence, which Zurg comes next?

a   b   a   b

2 How many spaceships will Zurg hit if he hits all the ones that come to an even number?

9-3   12-3   5+7

3 Which two badges are exactly the same?

 a

 b

 c

 d

66

Answers: 1) a. 2) Two. 3) b and d.

Red alert!

Buzz has called all the toys together to make sure that everyone is present and correct. Can you help Buzz spot which one of his friends is missing from the bottom picture?

Slinky Dog.

WHO ARE YOU?

Do you like going on adventures?

NO

YES

Do you have a friend that you do everything with?

NO

Do you like to be the leader?

YES

YES

Do you like telling jokes?

NO

Do you like learning new things?

YES

NO

Are you sporty?

YES

NO

NO

YES

MIKE

You're a loyal buddy who is always up for a laugh!

BUZZ

You're leader of the gang and always the first to try anything new!

Do you like to daydream?

YES

Do you like inventing things?

YES **NO**

Are you a bit of a show-off?

Do you like being on your own?

YES

YES **NO**

Do you like to talk a lot?

NO

Are you quite laid-back?

YES →

NO **YES**

Are you quite forgetful?

NO **YES**

FLIK

You're a dreamer who always sees the best in everything!

DORY

You're a great friend who everyone wants to hang around with!

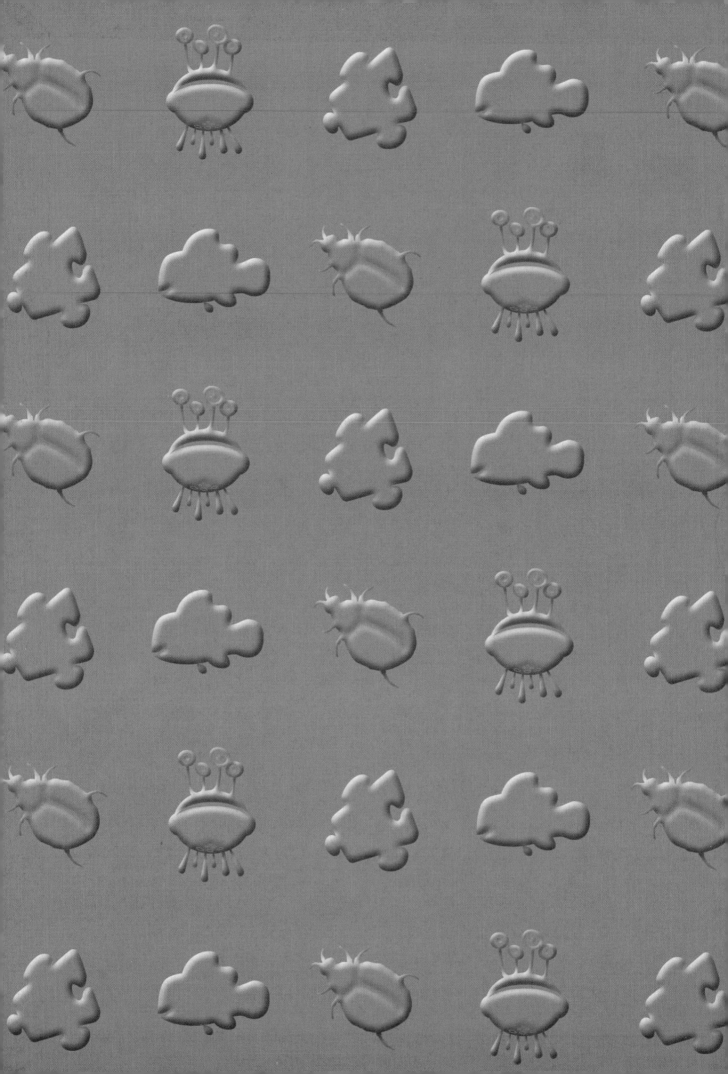